AUG 18 1992

ALSO BY DEBORAH KRASNER

♥

CELTIC:
Design and Style in Homes of Scotland, Ireland, and Wales

FROM
CELTIC
HEARTHS

FROM
CELTIC
HEARTHS

*Baked Goods
from Scotland, Ireland,
and Wales*

Text and illustrations by
DEBORAH KRASNER

V
VIKING
STUDIO
BOOKS

VIKING STUDIO BOOKS
Published by the Penguin Group
Viking Penguin, a division of Penguin Books USA Inc.,
375 Hudson Street, New York, New York 10014, U.S.A.
Penguin Books Ltd, 27 Wrights Lane,
London W8 5TZ, England
Penguin Books Australia Ltd, Ringwood,
Victoria, Australia
Penguin Books Canada Ltd, 10 Alcorn Avenue, Suite 300,
Toronto, Ontario, Canada M4V 3B2
Penguin Books (N.Z.) Ltd, 182–190 Wairau Road,
Auckland 10, New Zealand

Penguin Books Ltd. Registered Offices:
Harmondsworth, Middlesex, England

First published in 1991 by Viking Penguin,
a division of Penguin Books USA Inc.

1 3 5 7 9 10 8 6 4 2

Page 84 constitutes at extension of this copyright page.

CIP data available upon request

Printed in the United States of America
Set in Kennerley
Designed by Kathleen Herlihy-Paoli

This book is dedicated to my grandmothers,
who nurtured my interest in food:

in memory of my maternal grandmother,
Irene Roth Gould,

and in memory of my grandmother
by virtue of long affection,
Margaret Hanff

ACKNOWLEDGMENTS

First and foremost, I thank my agent, Amy Berkower of Writers House, who gave me the push that enabled this book to be imagined.

And then I thank my family—Michael, Abby, and Lizzie, who ate it all with pleasure and every evidence of good cheer!

Barbara Williams and Michael Fragnito have gladdened my fingers at keyboard and cookstove.

Thank you to Kathy Herlihy-Paoli, who always has stunning visual ideas.

Heartfelt thanks to all the cooks in my community who have worked their way through chapters, testing recipes in the heat of summer! Thank you to Mary Burke, Rosemary Ladd-Griffin, Andrea Darrow, Alice Halloran, Jessie Haas, Ann Pollina, and Debbie Wilson.

Finally, thanks to the many great cooks who have come before, who have made meals in hardship as well as delight, and who have passed their secrets on to us.

CONTENTS

FESTIVE ENDINGS:
Tea Cakes and Sweet Cakes 67

INTRODUCTION

I neither have an Irish grandmother nor a Welsh or
Scots one. In fact, there is no one in my whole family
who has any ancestral link with any region of the
Celtic fringe. But there are certain landscapes that
a traveler recognizes—a landscape that spells home
to some instinctive region within a person, a sense
of déjà vu when looking at the line of a hill rolling
and rippling across a field, the curve of a coastline,
and the way houses nestle and brood into landscape.
That sense of recognition, of comfort, of ease, is com-
pelling and urgent. It is a kind of falling in love.

Everyone knows that falling in love is obsessive,
a state of mind in which every detail of the beloved
wants exploring. Being country-enamored is no different. Besotted with Celtic landscape, I was drawn
into houses, and within houses I found stirring music
and the sweet, fresh smells of home baking.

This book is a collection of recipes for baked goods
from the Celtic regions. These delicious traditions
start from the garden, farmyard, and field—locally
grown grains; milk, and butter from the family cow;
honey from the bee skep; eggs from the coop—and
end up at the table as fragrant versions of the staff
of life. These scones, breads, cakes, and such were
the artful work of frugal women who used only what

foodstuffs were close to hand. Recipes were cherished, adapted, traded, and held, and when Famine, Clearance, and religious persecution reigned, the precious recipes were carried by immigrants to North America, Australia, and New Zealand, where they were used not only to nourish, but also to remind.

A note on terminology: in American terms, a scone is simply a baking-powder biscuit. But say "biscuit" to an Englishman, and he thinks "cookie." To muddle things further, a cookie to an Englishman is what we call a sweet bun! In addition, among the regions of the Celtic fringe, similar baked goods often have different names. Throughout this book, I have used the traditional Celtic names of foods.

On the subject of ingredients, there is much to say. Many of the most delicious traditional baked goods of the Celtic regions do not stint on butter and eggs, and sometimes feature lard and cream as well. However, although our lives today may be more sedentary and our daily fare more health-conscious, there will always be a place for special home-baked gems in our diet.

Happily, though, there are a number of recipes from these regions that promote arterial health, being high in fiber and low in fat and cholesterol. These worthy recipes are so designated in the book. And be assured that they are delicious too!

IN THE OVEN

Scones,
Oatcakes,
Farls

*I*n general, scones (and their close relations, oatcakes and farls) are absurdly easy to make, and take about fifteen to twenty minutes altogether from start to finish. (The rule with scones, as with all baking-powder biscuits, is to work as rapidly as possible to enable the chemical reaction to occur as fast as it can in the presence of heat.)

This speed of preparation makes scones perfect for a great many occasions beyond the traditional afternoon tea—I whip them up for breakfasts, brunches, and after-school treats.

Note, however, that in the recipes that follow the proportions of flour to liquid are elastic, as flours vary enormously and are profoundly affected by temperature, humidity, and atmospheric pressure. The point in all of these scone recipes is to make a dough that is wet and soft enough to roll, but not so soft that it sticks, yet firm enough to cut into shapes. So feel free to add more flour if the dough seems soft (kneading it rapidly on a floured board seems the best way to add it after the liquid has been absorbed). Conversely, if the dough is too stiff and dry to hold together after mixing in the required amount of liquid, add in a bit more liquid slowly until the dough feels workable. (Scone dough is much softer than yeast dough; it should almost flop onto the board, and can be patted into shape rather than rolled, if desired.)

SWEET MILK SCONES

This excellent basic scone recipe, along with its variations, comes from Catherine Brown's Glenfiddich Award–winning book, *Scottish Cookery*. Many scone recipes call for too much baking powder, which makes for too rapid a rise and leaves a baking-powder flavor. This recipe creates a single-acting baking powder by mixing baking soda and cream of tartar, producing a softer taste.

Note that the amounts of flour are elastic—flour is affected by weather conditions, and different days call for different flour amounts and degree of absorbency.

The variations listed below are traditional (and delicious), but don't be shy about making your own cross-cultural amendments. The Barking Radish, a catering company in Brattleboro, Vermont, makes wonderful scones with chopped crystallized ginger. And, to many Americans, chocolate chips are never unwelcome.

The savory variations on Sweet Milk Scones are excellent with soup. With the addition of a green salad, they make a fine meal.

2–3 cups unbleached flour
1 teaspoon baking soda
2 teaspoons cream of tartar
Salt to taste
4 tablespoons (½ stick) butter
¾ cup milk

Preheat the oven to 450°. Lightly grease a baking sheet and set aside.

Sift together the flour, soda, cream of tartar, and salt. Using a pastry blender or your hands, cut in the butter (or pulse in the food processor) until the mixture looks grainy, like coarse crumbs.

Pour the milk in a well in the center, and mix until a soft elastic dough is formed. (If using a food processor, be very careful not to overmix, as this produces a tough scone.)

Knead the dough lightly on a floured surface until smooth, and press with the hands or roll the dough into a pad about ¾ inch thick. (If the dough is rolled too thin, the scones don't rise properly.)

Cut into 2½- or 3-inch rounds with a glass or a cookie cutter, and bake on prepared sheet for about 10 minutes, or until they rise and are golden.

Yield: 8 scones

SWEET VARIATIONS

TREACLE SCONES

Prepare basic recipe for Sweet Milk Scones. Mix 2 table-spoons molasses into the milk before adding it to the flour. Add ½ cup chopped walnuts to the dough before rolling.

HONEY SCONES

Using basic recipe for Sweet Milk Scones, substitute ¼ cup orange juice and ½ cup milk for ¾ cup milk, and add 2 tablespoons honey, the grated zest of 1 lemon, and 1 tablespoon chopped walnuts to the dough before rolling it out.

JAM SCONES

Make the basic dough for Sweet Milk Scones and divide it in two. Roll out both pieces to ½-inch thickness, and form each into a large round or rectangle. Brush the edges of one piece with a beaten egg or with milk, and spread 2 tablespoons fruit jam to within an inch of the edge. Put the other piece of dough on top, and press lightly around the edges to secure the sandwich. Lightly score the top into squares, cutting only partway through; brush the top with beaten egg, and bake as above.

CREAM SCONES

Substitute ¾ cup fresh heavy cream or sour cream for the milk in the basic recipe. Add 2 eggs to the dough at the same time as the cream. This rich scone tastes quite different from the basic recipe, and can be used as a base for individual strawberry shortcakes.

FRUIT SCONES

Using basic Sweet Milk Scones recipe, add up to ½ cup of soft fruit such as blueberries, raspberries, sliced strawberries, or chopped mango along with a few spoonfuls of sugar if needed, to the dough before it is rolled out.

SAVORY VARIATIONS

HERB SCONES

Add 1 teaspoon dried herbs, or 2 teaspoons (or more) chopped fresh herbs, to the basic dough before rolling out. Tarragon is good with a chicken-based dish; basil or oregano are sublime with tomatoes; chopped cilantro and red pepper flakes make a spirited addition to soups of Asian or southwestern origin. For a truly intense herb scone, add ⅓ to ½ cup of pesto sauce to the dough along with the milk, keeping in mind that extra flour will be needed on the board to compensate for the extra liquid.

CHEESE SCONES

Add 1 generous cup of grated cheese to the basic dough before rolling it out. Cheddar is a particularly good choice, as is parmesan. These scones are so good they seriously threaten our children's allegiance to macaroni and cheese as the dinner of preference! I like to serve these scones with a vegetable soup.

ONION SCONES

Wilt 1 chopped smallish onion (Vidalia, for sweet flavor) in a pan with a little olive oil or canola oil (for health) or bacon fat (for tradition) until transparent but not brown. Cool. Add most of it to the dough before rolling it out, but for extra flavor reserve a bit of cooked onion to put on top of each scone (after brushing scone with beaten egg) before baking.

BARA CEIRCH

Welsh Oatcakes

Oatcakes are common to all of the regions of the Celtic fringe, and they can be quite tricky to make well. This completely reliable and easy recipe comes from the late and lamented Cuisinarts magazine, *The Pleasures of Cooking*. These oatcakes are crisp and savory, and they are utterly delicious when served with cheese.

2 cups rolled oats (not instant)
2 tablespoons unsalted butter
½ teaspoon salt
⅓ cup hot water

Preheat the oven to 350°.

In the bowl of a food processor fitted with a steel blade, combine 1½ cups of oats with the butter and salt. Process for about 20 seconds, until the mixture resembles coarse meal or flour.

With the motor running, add the hot water through the feed tube and process until combined (about 10 seconds).

Turn the dough out onto a surface sprinkled with about a third of the remaining ½ cup of oats. Flatten the dough into a 5-inch circle, sprinkle it with another third of the remaining oats, and roll out to a thickness of ⅛ inch.

Cut into 2½-inch circles with a glass or cookie cutter and place on a baking sheet sprinkled with the remaining oats. Reroll the scraps to make more circles.

Bake until edges are crisp and light brown, about 20–25 minutes.

Yield: 22 oatcakes

OAT FARLS

Farls, or round quarters of griddle-baked dough, are among the earliest and most primitive of baked goods. These farls, however, are oven-baked, and have an intriguing flavor that is all their own.

I have also made these farls using leftover cooked oatmeal, a use for which they were probably invented. Note that the only fat in them comes from buttermilk, which makes them a low-fat, low-cholesterol delicacy.

> 2 cups rolled oats (not instant)
> 1¼ to 2¼ cups buttermilk
> 2½ cups unbleached flour, sifted
> 1 teaspoon salt
> 1 teaspoon baking soda

The day before serving, mix the oats with 1¼ cups buttermilk. Cover with plastic wrap or a plate and let stand overnight at room temperature.

Preheat oven to 350°. Lightly grease a baking sheet and set aside.

Stir together the flour, salt, and baking soda. Gradually beat the flour mixture into the oat mixture to form a soft dough. Add more buttermilk if necessary.

Shape dough into a flattened circle about 1 inch thick. With a sharp knife, cut the dough into quarters. Place each farl, or quarter, on the prepared baking sheet and bake for about 40 minutes, or until browned.

Yield: 4 farls

These farls are low in fat, low in cholesterol, and high in fiber.

CURRANT AND CARAWAY SCONES

Currants and caraway seeds are a classic Celtic combination of ingredients. These extremely rich scones are the creation of Nantucket's famous cook Sarah Leah Chase, and I, as she does, always cut them with a 2½-inch heart-shaped cookie cutter.

> 4½ cups unbleached flour
> 2 teaspoons baking powder
> 1 teaspoon baking soda
> 3 tablespoons sugar
> 1 cup (2 sticks) cold unsalted butter, cut into small pieces
> 1¼ cups heavy cream
> 1 cup currants
> ¼ cup sweet Marsala wine

1 tablespoon caraway seeds
1 large egg
1 tablespoon water

Stir the flour, baking powder, soda, and sugar together in a large mixing bowl. Cut the butter into the flour mixture with a pastry blender until it looks grainy. Add the cream and mix with your hands until the dough holds together.

Place the currants and Marsala in a small pan and heat to boiling. Reduce the heat and simmer, stirring occasionally, for 2 minutes. Remove from heat and cool 10 minutes. Add the currants and liquid to the dough, then mix in the caraway seeds. Wrap dough in plastic wrap or wax paper and refrigerate for at least 1 hour.

Preheat the oven to 350°. Line two baking sheets with parchment paper.

Divide the dough in half. Roll out each half on a floured board to a thickness of ¾ inch. Cut with a 2- to 3-inch heart-shaped cutter and place the hearts 1 inch apart on the baking sheets. Mix the egg and water in a small bowl. Brush the egg wash over the top of each scone.

Bake the scones until light golden brown, about 15 minutes. Serve warm or at room temperature.

Yield: 36 heart-shaped scones

ROYAL HIBERNIAN
BROWN-BREAD SCONES

The Royal Hibernian is an elegant hotel in Dublin. Afternoon tea is served in the grand tradition, and these excellent scones are always one of the star features on the tray.

2 cups unbleached flour
1 teaspoon baking powder
1 teaspoon baking soda
½ teaspoon salt
2 cups whole-wheat flour
2 tablespoons sugar
6 tablespoons (¾ stick) cold unsalted butter, cut
* into small pieces*
1½ to 1¾ cups cold milk

Preheat the oven to 375°. Lightly grease and flour a baking sheet and set aside.

Sift together the unbleached flour, baking powder, soda, and salt. Sift in the whole-wheat flour, and mix in the sugar. Using your hands, a pastry blender, or the steel blade of a food processor, cut in the butter until the mixture looks grainy.

Stir in 1½ cups milk until the mixture forms a soft dough.

Add more milk if necessary.

Turn dough out onto a floured board and roll to a thickness of ½ inch. Cut into 2-inch rounds with a glass or cookie cutter, place on prepared baking sheet, and bake for 20 minutes.

Yield: 15 scones

BOXTY BREAD

Boxty is to some Irish bards what madeleines were to Proust—food, inspiration, and the key to memory. There is a wonderful and sprightly sentimental Irish ballad called "Colcannon," which is an ode to Irish food and which devotes a full verse to the pleasures of boxty:

> *Well, did you ever take potato cake and boxty
> to the school
> Tucked underneath your oxter with your books,
> your slate, and rule
> And when teacher wasn't lookin' sure a great
> big bite you'd take
> Of the creamy flavored soft and meltin' sweet
> potato cake.*

Boxty refers to both the food and the implement used to make it—both the finished potato dish as well as the homemade graters made from empty metal tins or boxes on which the potatoes are shredded. Boxty cakes are made on the griddle, and are a kind of potato pancake. Boxty bread is oven-baked.

2 pounds large red-skinned California potatoes (or 1 pound potatoes and 2 cups leftover mashed potatoes)
4 cups unbleached flour
Salt and pepper to taste
¼ cup (½ stick) unsalted butter, melted

Preheat the oven to 375°. Lightly grease a baking sheet and set aside.

Wash the potatoes well and divide them into two portions. Boil one portion about 25 minutes, or until done, then mash them. (Alternatively, leftover mashed potatoes can be substituted.)

While the first portion of potatoes is boiling, peel the other portion of potatoes and grate them coarsely. Place these grated potatoes in a clean tea towel and wring them over a bowl to collect the juices. Mix the drained grated raw potatoes with the mashed potatoes.

The bowl that has the potato juice should have a watery

liquid on the top and white starch at the bottom. Pour off the water and add the starch to the potato mixture.

Sift the flour, salt, and pepper together over the potatoes 1 cup at a time, mixing well after each addition. Add ¼ cup melted butter, then turn dough onto a floured board and knead lightly.

Form dough into 4 flat rounds about 1 inch thick. Score each round into quarters, cutting only partway through so that each farl can be broken off after baking.

Bake on prepared sheet for 20 minutes. Reduce heat to 350° and bake for an additional 45 minutes, or until brown on top and cooked inside.

Serve hot, splitting each farl off the round, and then further splitting each horizontally (with a fork as for an English muffin). If you are a traditionalist, slather each half with butter.

Yield: 16 farls from 4 small round loaves

ON THE GRIDDLE

Drop Scones,
Pikelets,
Bannocks

Scots say "girdle," which has a nice ring, and many households had affectionate names for the flat iron cooking pan that functioned as oven and broiler when cooking on a hearth. If you are lucky, you can still find old iron girdles at antique stores and flea markets that carry nineteenth-century goods. New griddles, however, are still being made, in heavy stovetop versions as well as Teflon-coated electric countertop models. If there is no griddle to hand, a heavy cast-iron frying pan works nearly as well, provided it has been well seasoned.

PIKELETS

To an American, pikelets are pancakes served as bread. Served warm from the griddle, accompanied by butter and jam, they are an unusual and tasty teatime treat.

> 1 cup unbleached flour
> 1/8 teaspoon baking soda
> 1/8 teaspoon salt
> 3 tablespoons sugar
> 2/3 cup buttermilk
> 1 egg, lightly beaten
> 2 teaspoons unsalted butter, melted and cooled

Preheat a 12-inch seasoned cast-iron frying pan or large griddle over high heat.

Sift together the flour, baking soda, and salt into a large bowl. Stir in the sugar. Add the buttermilk, egg, and melted butter, and mix well with a wooden spoon.

Grease the griddle with butter or oil. Drop tablespoonfuls of batter on the griddle, spacing pikelets well apart (about 6 will fit). Cook until tops are bubbling and undersides are golden brown, about 5 minutes. Flip over and cook until done on the other side.

As the scones are cooked, keep them warm wrapped in a cloth. Serve warm with butter.

Yield: 12 to 15 pancake-like scones

PRATIE SCONES

Pratie is what potatoes are called in parts of Ireland and Scotland, and these paper-thin, almost pancake-like scones are an excellent example of one of the many delicious dishes that can be made from them.

I first saw pratie scones when I was invited to an elegant lunch in rural Scotland, where they were passed around cold in a serving dish as bread. Later on, while traveling around Scotland, I saw them sold ready-made in packages in shops. When made at home, however, they are most delicious served warm from the griddle. We like them as a special treat for a weekend lunch.

1 cup warm mashed potatoes
⅓ cup melted butter
1 teaspoon salt
½ cup sifted all-purpose flour

Preheat a 12-inch seasoned cast-iron frying pan or griddle over moderate heat.

Mix together all ingredients until thoroughly blended. Turn the dough out onto a floured board and divide into thirds. Roll out each third into a circle about ¼ inch thick. Score each circle into 6 wedges.

Sprinkle the griddle with flour and bake each circle for about 5 minutes, until edges begin to brown, turning once to cook both sides. Serve hot or cold.

Yield: 18 scones

BRUNNIES

Brunnie is the Scottish name for these delicious griddle scones, which have a delicate texture when made with the requisite haste. Serve them hot, split, and coated with whatever your conscience dictates (tradition demands butter and jam). Like English muf-fins, which these brunnies resemble except for shape, leftovers can be split and toasted.

2 cups unbleached flour
1 teaspoon cream of tartar
1 teaspoon baking soda
½ teaspoon salt
1 teaspoon sugar
⅓–½ cup buttermilk

Preheat a 12-inch seasoned cast-iron frying pan or large griddle over moderate heat.

Sift together the flour, cream of tartar, baking soda, salt, and sugar. Mix half of this mixture with enough butter-milk to form a soft dough.

Turn dough out onto a floured surface and pat into a circle about ½ inch thick. Cut the dough in 8 or 10 wedges, and bake on the griddle until lightly browned (about 5 minutes). Turn to brown on the other side.

Repeat the process with the other half of the dry and wet ingredients.

Yield: 8 to 10 brunnies or scones

These brunnies are low in fat and cholesterol.

SINGING HINNIES

These marvelous scones have an onomatopoeic name—it comes from the sound you hear as they cook, when the butter, cream, and lard melt and sizzle in contact with the hot griddle!

1½ cups unbleached flour
½ teaspoon salt
1 teaspoon baking powder
4 tablespoons (½ stick) butter
4 tablespoons lard
⅔ cup buttermilk
⅓ cup heavy cream
3 tablespoons currants

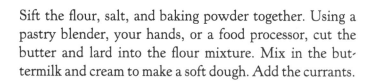

Preheat a seasoned 12-inch cast-iron frying pan or a griddle over moderately high heat. Grease lightly.

Sift the flour, salt, and baking powder together. Using a pastry blender, your hands, or a food processor, cut the butter and lard into the flour mixture. Mix in the buttermilk and cream to make a soft dough. Add the currants.

Roll out the dough onto a floured board to a thickness of about ¾ inch. Cut into 2- to 3-inch rounds with a glass or cookie cutter. Bake on the griddle (listening closely for the singing) until the underside is browned, then turn and bake the other side until done.

Serve warm.

Yield: 12 to 16 scones

PRATIE OATEN

Irish cook and author Malachi McCormick says this is a favorite Northern Irish teatime (or breakfast) dish. Although very plain, the combination of oats and potatoes is, I think, an inspired one.

3 large potatoes
1 cup rolled oats (not instant)
½ cup (1 stick) unsalted butter, melted
1 teaspoon salt
1–2 tablespoons vegetable oil, butter, or bacon fat

Boil the potatoes in their skins until done, about 25 minutes. Peel, mash, and cool.

Mix in the oats to form a soft dough. Add the melted butter and salt and mix well.

Roll out the dough on a floured board to a thickness of ½ inch. Cut into 2½-inch rounds with a glass or cookie cutter.

Heat the oil, butter, or bacon fat (the traditional choice) in a cast-iron skillet and fry until golden brown, about 5 minutes per side. Serve warm.

Yield: 22 scones

BERE BANNOCKS

This is one of the most winsome recipes in this collection—high in fiber and entirely without fat, easy to make and delicious to eat. *Bere* means barley, and bannocks like these were daily fare for residents of the Hebrides and Orkney islands.

These rounds are in shape and in texture much like what Americans call English muffins, and they can also be made in large batches and frozen. If not eaten fresh from the pan, they are very good split horizontally and toasted.

1½ cups warm water
1 teaspoon molasses or maple syrup
1 cup barley flour (available in health food stores)

¼ cup self-rising flour (self-rising flour can be
made at home by adding 1½ teaspoons baking
powder and ½ teaspoon salt to 1 cup all-
purpose flour)
1½ teaspoons baking powder
½ teaspoon salt

Preheat a 12-inch seasoned frying pan or any size griddle over medium heat.

Mix ½ cup of water with the molasses or syrup. Sift the dry ingredients together over a large bowl (the barley flour will leave a sawdust-like fiber residue in the bottom of the sifter that increases the fiber content when added to the dough). Stir in the liquid to make a soft dough, adding as much as 1 cup of additional water if necessary.

Turn the dough out onto a floured board and flour your hands. Gently form the dough into 6 balls. Flatten each ball to ½-inch thickness. Sprinkle the griddle with flour and cook all the bannocks at once until the undersides are brown (about 10 minutes). Flip over and cook the other side.

Serve warm, split open to receive whatever spread you choose.

Yield: 6 3-inch rounds

These bannocks are low in fat, low in cholesterol, and high in fiber.

COTTAGE ROUNDS

Soda-Risen Breads

*I*rish soda breads are perhaps the most well-known of Celtic culinary contributions, although they are by no means limited to Ireland alone. Soda breads are marvelous to have in one's cooking repertoire because they are so easy to throw together, require no rising time, and are quick to bake.

There have been many times when I've found myself in circumstances where bread was needed within the hour to feed a hungry family (in a remote district of Nova Scotia, Canada, where the only bread to buy was spongelike packaged white; snowed in by a heavy Vermont blizzard, with the road impassable; in a rented cabin, with a store many miles off). In these situations, I have been glad to have a soda bread recipe firmly inscribed in memory. And the smell of bread baking is always an added bonus.

One of the saddest and most telling discoveries one can make, when tracing recipes from points of origin in the British Isles across the Atlantic to American cookbooks, is that Yankee versions of old-country dishes tend to have added to them immense amounts of butter, eggs, and sugar. Perhaps it was that people recently arrived felt so newly prosperous, at least on the basic foodstuff level, that they were proud of their ability to fancy up and enrich the old recipes. Thus soda breads, which in their home countries are a real bread, tend in American recipes to be cakes, no matter what they are titled.

For reasons of flavor as well as health, and in the interests of tradition, the soda breads that follow are all real breads, although some variations on them, like toasted bran, or flour mixed with oats, are more modern additions.

TOASTED BRAN BREAD BOLUISCE

This unusual and full-flavored variation on soda bread is from Boluisce's Seafood Bar at Spiddal, in Galway. The special taste of toasted bran is a unique addition to the soda bread theme.

- 3 cups wheat bran (kept refrigerated)
- 5 cups whole-wheat flour (preferably organic stone-ground)
- 2 cups yogurt
- 2 cups milk
- 2 teaspoons baking soda
- 3 teaspoons salt
- 2 teaspoons sugar
- 2 teaspoons baking powder

Preheat the oven to 400°, and arrange the bran on a baking sheet in a single layer. Toast until dark brown (about 15 to 20 minutes). When done, add to the whole wheat flour and mix well. Stir in the yogurt.

Pour the milk into a medium-size bowl, and then add the soda, salt, sugar, and baking powder. Stir to dissolve. Add this liquid mixture to the flour mixture and mix well (this is a very wet dough). Turn out onto a floured board and knead lightly.

Divide dough into two portions, and shape each into a round loaf. Cut a cross in the top with the tip of a sharp knife, and set the loaves on a greased baking sheet.

Bake for 35 to 40 minutes, or until the loaves sound hollow when thumped on the bottom.

Yield: 2 cottage loaves

BALLYMALOE BREAD

Ballymaloe is the name of a wonderful country-house hotel owned by Myrtle Allen and her family in Shanagarry, County Cork. Ms. Allen's food is famous all over Ireland, and, thanks to her cookbook, now is known in many more parts of the world. Her daughter-in-law, Darina Allen, is carrying on Ballymaloe's culinary tradition with a cooking school as well as a cooking program on Irish television.

Ballymaloe soda bread is my personal favorite of all soda breads—I think it is the best soda bread I have ever tasted, and although I make it often, I never tire of it.

Finally, note that the only possible fat in this recipe would come from yogurt, for which you could substitute the lowfat or nonfat variety, or buttermilk.

4 cups whole-wheat flour
1 cup unbleached white flour
½ cup rolled oats
1½ teaspoons baking soda
1 teaspoon salt
2–3 cups buttermilk or unflavored yogurt

Preheat the oven to 475°. Lightly grease a baking sheet and set aside.

In a large mixing bowl, stir together the flours, oats, baking soda, and salt until well combined.

Using a wooden spoon, gradually beat in 2 cups of buttermilk or yogurt. (If the dough is too stiff to knead, add more buttermilk or yogurt.) This should be a fairly soft dough, less stiff than a yeast dough. Turn out on a floured board and knead lightly.

Divide the dough into thirds and shape each into a round loaf about 4 inches in diameter. Score the tops of each loaf into quarters, and place on the prepared sheet.

Bake for 15 minutes, then reduce heat to 400° and bake loaves 15 to 20 minutes longer, or until they are browned and sound hollow when tapped.

Yield: 3 small cottage loaves

This bread is low in fat, low in cholesterol, and high in fiber.

IRON-POT OVEN SCONE

Many attempts have been made to duplicate the qualities of heat and humidity found in the old clay beehive ovens that were built into chimneys and heated by wood. One close approximation can be made using a covered cast-iron casserole or Dutch oven. If you haven't got a cast-iron casserole, a ceramic one will do almost as well. Do be sure, however, that the top is as wide or wider than the base, so that the finished bread can be removed. The lid should fit closely, to allow the steam to moisten the rising bread. If the pot is not well seasoned, grease it well.

Again, note that the only fat in this recipe comes from buttermilk.

> 2 cups unbleached flour
> 1 teaspoon baking soda
> 1 teaspoon cream of tartar
> 1 teaspoon salt
> 1 cup buttermilk

Preheat the oven to 450°.

Sift the flour, along with the baking soda, cream of tartar, and salt, into a mixing bowl. Make a well in the center and add the buttermilk. Mix until dough is a soft and elastic consistency. Turn dough out onto a floured board, knead very lightly, and form it into a round.

Place dough in the iron pot and cover. Bake until risen and dry, about 30 to 35 minutes. Keep bread warm in a towel if not serving immediately.

Yield: 1 good-size cottage loaf

These scones are low in fat and cholesterol.

IRISH WHEATMEAL SODA BREAD

This recipe comes from Elizabeth David's marvelous work, *English Bread and Yeast Cookery*. Ms. David got the recipe from Gracie McDermot, who cooks for artist Derek Hill. It has a good and honest flavor, and is very easy to make.

1 cup unbleached white flour
2 cups whole-wheat flour
½ teaspoon salt
1 teaspoon baking powder
About 1 cup buttermilk

Preheat the oven to 450°.

Sift the flours together with the salt and baking powder into a mixing bowl. Make a well in the center and pour in the buttermilk. Stir to mix well.

Turn the dough out onto a lightly floured board and lightly pat it into a round loaf. Put the loaf into a buttered cast-iron skillet and bake for 10 minutes, or until the bread has risen and is slightly browned. Lower the heat to 375° and bake for an additional 25 minutes, or until done.

Yield: 1 round loaf

This bread is low in fat, low in cholesterol, and high in fiber.

WHOLE-WHEAT SODA BREAD

Uncompromising, full of whole-wheat flavor and fiber, this one-hundred-percent-whole-wheat loaf is most delectable when just cooled, but is also very good toasted.

This baking method, in which the loaves are baked inside an inverted deep baking tin, is another way to duplicate the lift achieved with the old brick-lined wood-fired bread ovens. It works very well.

1 *level teaspoon baking soda*
2 *teaspoons salt*
3–3¾ *cups whole-wheat flour (preferably stone-*
  ground)
1¼ *cups cold buttermilk*
2–4 *tablespoons warm water*

Preheat the oven to 450°.

Sift the soda and salt together with the flour, making sure all ingredients are well distributed. Add the buttermilk and mix, adding warm water if the dough is too dry.

Form the dough quickly into two loaves that are as tall as you can make them. Place them on a floured baking sheet, and cover each loaf with a deep, at least 6 or 7 inches high, cake tin (springform pans do very well), or a clean earthenware flowerpot with the hole blocked by aluminum foil.

Immediately set on the center shelf of the oven and bake for 30 minutes. Remove the covering tins and bake the loaves another 10 to 15 minutes, until the crust is browned but not overbaked.

Yield: 2 round loaves

This bread is low in fat, low in cholesterol, and high in fiber.

COUNTRY LOAVES

Yeast Breads,
Baps,
Rolls

There are two strands of tradition within Celtic baking—one is that of breads: strong, honest loaves good for slicing. The other tradition comes from festive foods, from holiday celebrations that marked points on the calendar of the religious and agricultural year. This second tradition is sometimes called a "lardy cake" tradition, because these breads were made with precious commodities such as butter and lard, and were eaten only on those special occasions.

It's good to remember the specialness of these cakes, because their richness and lavish use of animal fats would give pause to anyone concerned with nutrition. However, as an only-on-special-occasions treat, they are quite worth cooking and eating, and there is something terribly gratifying about keeping these old recipes alive and in use.

BARA GWENITH
Welsh Wholemeal Bread

This is one of the simplest yeast bread recipes I know, and is ideal for the beginning yeast cook. If you have a large-bowl food processor, it is possible to make this from start to finish in slightly more than an hour, with only about 5 or 10 minutes of that being actual preparation time. The secret to this speed is a double helping of yeast and only one rising. (If using a food processor, just do all the adding and mixing in the machine.)

> 1 teaspoon salt
> 9–10 cups whole-wheat flour (preferably stone-ground)
> 2 tablespoons unsalted butter
> 2 tablespoons active dry yeast (2 packages)
> 3 cups warm water
> 1 tablespoon brown sugar

In a large mixing bowl, or the bowl of a large capacity food processor fitted with a plastic blade, combine the salt and flour and cut in the butter. Dissolve the yeast in water and stir in the sugar.

Pour the yeast mixture into the flour mixture and knead (or process) until the dough is smooth and elastic.

Divide the dough into two portions, shape each into a loaf, and place in two greased 8½ × 4½-inch loaf tins. Cover with a clean tea towel and let rise until doubled in bulk, about 30 minutes. Preheat the oven to 400°.

Bake for 35 to 40 minutes, or until the loaves sound hollow when thumped. Turn out onto a rack and cool.

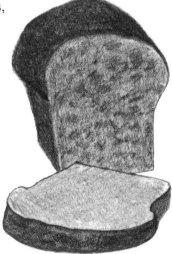

Yield: 2 loaves

BARM BRACK

This bread, as well as *Bara Brith* and Selkirk Bannock, are breads in the "lardy cake" tradition. Their origins are quite old, and today are still linked with holidays. Barm brack is served all over Ireland on All Hallows Eve, and usually contains charms and coins baked in the batter to foretell the future.

Although these breads are similar, and speak eloquently of their common Celtic ancestry, they each have their own special appeal. I once baked all three the same day, and asked a group of friends to choose their favorites. There was no winner—the votes were evenly divided!

This recipe is my own adaptation, using some elements from Bernard Clayton's formula and some from Elizabeth David's.

> 2½ teaspoons active dry yeast or one package
> 1¼–1½ cups combined equal amounts of
>   lukewarm water and milk
> 3 teaspoons salt
> 4–5 cups unbleached flour
> ½ cup (1 stick) butter
> ¾ cup sugar
> 3 eggs
> ½ cup caraway seeds

1 teaspoon allspice
½ teaspoon mace
½ cup currants
¼ cup minced dried apricots
Minced zest of 1 lemon

Dissolve the yeast in the water/milk mixture. Mix the salt with the flour, make a well in the center, and pour in the yeast mixture. Stir. Melt the butter and add it to the dough along with the sugar, then beat in the eggs, one at a time.

Add the caraway seeds and spices. Knead in as much extra flour as necessary to make a good dough, and continue kneading until smooth and elastic.

Form dough into a round ball and place in a greased bowl. Let rise, covered, in a warm, draft-free place until double in bulk (about 1 hour). Punch dough down, turn out onto a lightly floured board, and knead in the fruit. (If you add a little cornstarch to the fruit, it doesn't stick together and goes more easily into the dough.)

Grease a cast-iron or clay casserole or a baking pan with a 2-quart capacity. Shape the dough and let it rise again, covered with a cloth, in the baking pan for about half an hour, or until doubled in bulk. Preheat the oven to 375°.

Bake 45 minutes to 1 hour, or until the bread sounds hollow when thumped. Turn out on a rack to cool. The bread can be garnished with confectioner's sugar sifted over the top.

Yield: 1 large loaf

BARA BRITH
Speckled Bread

This is a Welsh spiced and fruited sweet bread. It is quite delicious plain as well as toasted.

2½ cups unbleached flour
½ cup whole-wheat flour
1 teaspoon salt
⅔ cup milk
1 teaspoon active dry yeast or less than 1 package
6 tablespoons butter
¼ cup sugar
½ cup raisins or sultanas
½ cup currants
1½ tablespoons chopped dried apricots or
    candied citrus peel
½ teaspoon allspice

Combine the flours and salt in a ceramic or metal bowl

and warm in the oven for a few minutes. Warm the milk to a little over 100° and add the yeast to it. Cut the butter into small pieces and stir it in the warm milk mixture until melted. Pour this into the flour mixture and form into a fairly light dough. Transfer to an oiled bowl, cover with a clean towel, and let rise until doubled in bulk, about 30 to 40 minutes if all the ingredients were warm to start with.

Mix together the sugar, dried fruits, and allspice and put them in the oven to warm as well. After a few minutes, work this mixture into the dough with your hands, trying to be sure that all ingredients are well distributed. If the dough seems stiff, add additional milk as necessary.

Grease a large 1½- to 2-quart casserole or an oversize loaf pan that has outward-sloping sides. Warm it in the oven and pat the dough into the pan to fit. Cover with plastic wrap or a clean towel and let the dough rise to the top of the pan, about 1 to 1½ hours.

Preheat the oven to 425°. Bake on the center shelf for 20 to 30 minutes, covering the top with aluminum foil during the last 10 minutes of cooking.

Cool the loaf in the pan for 5 to 10 minutes, then turn out to cool on a wire rack.

Yield: 1 large loaf

SELKIRK BANNOCK

Finally, the Scottish version of a lardy cake with fruit, still made with lard mixed with butter. Because it is so rich, it should be sliced thinly. It is an excellent keeper, and well wrapped in an airtight tin, it is a good choice for a food gift to send to faraway friends.

> 4–5 cups unbleached flour
> 2½ teaspoons active dry yeast (or 1 package)
> 1½ cups hot water
> 2 teaspoons salt
> 1 cup sweet butter (2 sticks), at room
>   temperature
> ½ cup lard, at room temperature
> 1 cup sugar
> 2 pounds raisins, or 1 pound raisins and 1 pound
>   chopped dried apricots and whole currants
> (optional) chopped zest of one orange

In a large food processor fitted with the plastic blade, pulse together 2½ cups flour, yeast, and salt. Add the hot water and pulse to combine. (In a mixer or by hand, mix the salt, yeast, and hot water into 1 cup of flour).

In a separate bowl, cream the lard, butter, and sugar together. Combine with the flour mixture (by hand or mixer), or by pulsing in the food processor.

(All methods) Add more flour, ½ cup at a time, until the mixture is a smooth and elastic dough. In the food processor, it will ride the blade and clean the container.

Add the dried fruit and orange peel, if using. (Knead the fruit into the dough by hand or by machine, kneading until the dough is very smooth and elastic, about 8 minutes. Add small amounts of flour as necessary.) In the food processor, knead by pulsing until the fruit seems evenly distributed and the dough elastic, about 1 minute.

Divide the dough into three portions, shape into rounds, and place in greased 8″ round cake pans, or cast iron frying pans. Cover with waxed paper, and let rise at room temperature for half an hour.

Twenty minutes before baking, preheat the oven to 350°.

Using the oven's middle shelf, bake for 1–1½ hours, or until the loaves sound hollow when thumped. If the crust seems to be browning too much, it can be covered with a piece of foil or brown paper bag.

Cool on a metal rack completely before wrapping.

Yield: 3 round loaves

BAPS

Baps are the national roll of Scotland, where they are also known as "morning rolls" or "fadge." Round, white, and floury, they have a wonderful taste and fragrance. Like all baked goods, they freeze well.

> 2 scant teaspoons active dry yeast (or less than 1
>   package)
> ⅔ cup lukewarm milk, plus extra for finishing
> ⅔ cup lukewarm water
> 2 teaspoons salt
> 3 cups unbleached flour, plus extra for finishing

Dissolve the yeast in the milk and water in a medium bowl. Sift the salt with the flour into a large bowl. Pour the well-mixed wet mixture into the dry mixture and stir. If this dough is too stiff, add a little more milk. Turn out onto a floured board and knead lightly. Place dough in an oiled bowl, cover with a clean towel, and let rise in a warm place for about 1½ hours.

Flour a baking sheet. Punch down the dough and divide it into 8 or 9 portions. Form these into ovals, and set them on the baking sheet, leaving as much room as possible between them. Cover with plastic wrap touching the dough to prevent a skin from forming and let them sit for 15 minutes to rise again. Preheat the oven to 425°.

Brush the tops and sides of the baps with milk, then sprinkle with flour. With a floury finger, make a deepish impression in the center of each bap. Bake on the center shelf of the oven for 15 to 20 minutes, or until puffed and just golden. More flour can be sifted over the finished baps if desired. Serve warm.

Yield: 8 to 9 rolls

CORNISH SPLITS

These plain dinner rolls originated in Cornwall, another ancient Celtic region. Thanks to Elizabeth David's tireless research into traditional English cookery, we know that they are sometimes served with a dusting of granulated sugar poured over their tops before baking, and served as a sweet roll. Another old recipe uses them as a base for a dinner dish of melted cheese and red wine, or melted cheese and ale (not unlike the classic Welsh Rabbit).

Elizabeth David quotes Kathleen Thomas, author of *A West Country Cookery Book,* as saying that splits eaten with cream and treacle (molasses) are known as "thunder and lightning."

1 teaspoon active dry yeast (or slightly less than
  half a package)
1¼ cups lukewarm milk
1 tablespoon sugar
3 cups unbleached flour
¼ teaspoon salt
2 tablespoons unsalted butter, melted and cooled

In a small bowl, dissolve the yeast in the milk and add the sugar. Sift the flour and salt together into a large mixing bowl and add the cooled melted butter.

Add the yeast mixture to the flour mixture, turn out onto a floured board, and knead to a smooth dough. Place the dough in an oiled bowl, cover with a clean tea towel, and let rise in a warm, draft-free place for 45 minutes.

Turn dough out onto the freshly floured board and shape into 6 or 7 balls. Place dough balls in a buttered and floured 9-inch-square baking tin. Let them sit, covered, for 15 minutes to rise again. Preheat the oven to 425°.

Bake 15 to 20 minutes, or until browned and puffed. Split open and serve warm.

Yield: 6 to 7 rolls

ABERDEEN ROWIES

Rowies, also called Butteries, are a miracle! Made from a yeast dough that is rolled out, spread with butter, folded, re-rolled, and spread again and again, they are a training course for puff pastry, Celtic style. Although similar to croissants, they are less rich and much easier to make. What emerges from the oven is a homely square of layered pastry, golden brown and flavored with butter.

These rowies freeze beautifully, and can be easily reheated under an inverted cake tin in a low oven.

> 1 teaspoon active dry yeast (or less than 1
>   package)
> 1 cup lukewarm water
> 2¼ cups unbleached flour
> 2 teaspoons salt
> ¾ cup (1½ sticks) cold unsalted butter
> 1 cup cornstarch (or more if necessary)

Dissolve the yeast in the water in a medium bowl. Sift the flour and the salt together into a large bowl. Add the yeast mixture gradually, making a medium-soft dough. Turn dough out onto a floured board, and form it into a ball. Place in a bowl and cover with a clean towel. Let rise in a warm, draft-free place for 30–45 minutes.

Divide the butter into two portions, each cut into tiny cubes. On a freshly floured board, punch down the dough and knead it, then dust the board with cornstarch. Roll out the dough into a 10 × 8-inch rectangle. Spread half the butter cubes (which should be cold but not hard) almost, but not quite, to the edges of the rectangle.

Fold the dough over in thirds, as you would a business letter, and roll lightly back into a rectangle. Turn the mass sideways, fold in thirds again, and roll again. Repeat this turning, folding, and rolling one more time. Let the dough rest for 15 minutes, preferably in the refrigerator, wrapped in wax paper.

Again, roll the dough into a rectangle on a freshly dusted board, spread with the remainder of the butter cubes, and repeat the three turns and folds. Again, let the dough rest in the refrigerator for 15 to 30 minutes.

Finally, roll out the dough into a rectangle once more, making it as neat and as even as possible. With a sharp knife, cut the dough into 24 squares as uniform in size as possible. (But don't worry if they are not perfectly sized; this is part of their homemade charm. Any very large squares can be cut diagonally into triangles.)

Preheat the oven to 425°. Arrange the rowies on baking sheets dusted with cornstarch. Cover with wax paper or plastic wrap and let stand for 30 minutes (but not in too warm a place or the butter will melt).

Bake for 15 to 20 minutes, or until pale golden and popped. Serve warm for breakfast.

Yield: 24 to 30 flaky rolls

SMALL CAKES

Cookies,
Shortbreads,
Sweet Biscuits

A case could certainly be made that short-breads are Scotland's claim to food immortality. Sublime and buttery, they have a flavor that just demands repeated nibbles. I certainly think they are a wonderful sweet and had trouble choosing which ones to include in this collection, as every variation I tried seemed better than the one before. After much soul- and palate-searching, I have included three that I think are the best. But other regions of the Celtic fringe have their own unique cookies, and I have included some very special recipes from Wales as well.

TEISENNAU FFAIR LLANDDAROG

Llanddarog Fair Cakes

Originally popular at the turn of the century in rural Wales, these cakes were country-fair treats. Llanddarog ("Ll" is pronounced "th" in Welsh) is near Carmarthen. This recipe is adapted for American ingredients from *Lamb, Leeks, and Laverbread*, a Welsh cookbook by Gilli Davies, and the haunting flavor of these cakes makes friends often request the recipe when I make it for them.

> ½ pound (2 sticks) unsalted butter
> 1½ cups self-rising flour (see page 25)
> ¾ cup confectioner's sugar, plus more for
>   dredging
> ½ cup currants
> 3 tablespoons dark beer, ale, or stout

Preheat the oven to 350°. Lightly grease a baking sheet and set aside.

Cut the butter into the flour with a pastry blender, then add the sugar and currants.

Slowly add enough beer to make a soft dough. Turn it

out onto a floured board and roll to a thickness of ¼ inch.

Cut into 2-inch rounds with a glass or cookie cutter and bake for 15 to 20 minutes, or until edges start to brown and the aroma fills the kitchen. Cool on wire racks and dust with confectioner's sugar.

Yield: 20 cookies

MONTROSE CAKES

These delicate little cakes are flavored with rose water, which can be found in Indian food stores. The cakes' old-fashioned aroma and taste is something like that of a rose-flavored pound cake. I bake them in madeleine pans, which gives them a shallow, shell-shaped form. They can also be made in mini-muffin tins or in the bottoms of regular-size muffin tins.

½ cup (1 stick) unsalted butter, softened
½ cup sugar
3 eggs
⅓ cup currants
2 teaspoons brandy
2 teaspoons rose water
½ cup self-rising flour (see page 25)
Pinch of freshly grated nutmeg

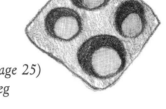

Preheat the oven to 375°. Grease a madeleine pan or two mini-muffin pans and set aside.

Cream the butter and sugar together. Add the eggs one at a time, beating well after each addition.

Stir in the currants, brandy, and rose water and mix thoroughly.

Sift the flour and nutmeg together, then add to the butter mixture.

Scrape batter into the prepared tins, filling them no more than half full.

Bake for 10 to 15 minutes, or until the edges are brown.

Yield: 20 small cakes

TELEGRAPH HOUSE SCOTTISH OATCAKES

These are the most incredible cookies—no one who has ever tasted them has failed to ask for the recipe. One visitor said that she didn't know you could make cookies like this at home! Their robust flavor is some-thing like English digestive biscuits, only better. The thinner they are when baked, the crisper and better they taste. I've included several alternative ways to shape them, as rolling them thin can be tricky. As you can see, these oatcakes are the sweet version of the savory Welsh oatcakes (see page 7).

Telegraph House is in San Francisco, and their recipe was printed one day in *The New York Times*.

½ teaspoon baking soda
½ cup boiling water
1 cup sugar
2 cups rolled oats (not instant)
2 cups unbleached flour
2 cups wheat bran
1 teaspoon salt
1¼ cups (2½ sticks) butter

Preheat the oven to 350°.

Dissolve the baking soda in the boiling water and let stand until cool.

Combine all of the dry ingredients in a large bowl (or the bowl of a food processor) and cut in the butter. Add the baking soda mixture. If using a processor, pulse until the dough rides the blade. If by hand, work in with a fork and then gently knead in the bowl for a few seconds.

Turn the dough out on a floured board and roll as thinly as possible, to a thickness of about ⅛ inch. Cut into 2-inch squares and transfer to a greased baking sheet.

Or, roll the dough into a long sausage shape, wrap with plastic wrap, and freeze for at least a few hours. Using a sharp serrated knife, carefully cut very thin slices of cold dough and transfer them to a greased baking sheet.

Or, form the dough into tablespoon-size balls, place on a greased baking sheet, and press down with a fork or the bottom of a glass that's been dipped in cornstarch to prevent sticking. Press down evenly to make a thin cookie.

Bake for 10 to 15 minutes. (If the dough is thicker than ⅛ inch when raw, the cookies will need more time to cook.) They are done when the edges are brown and crisp and the kitchen is fragrant. Cool on wire racks.

Yield: 8 to 9 dozen

TEISEN LAP
Welsh Butter Cakes

These butter cakes are in fact a fried cookie—sort of a cross between a crumpet and a small cake. They are very unusual and extremely good.

> 2¼ cups flour
> ¾ cup sugar
> 1½ teaspoons allspice
> 1 teaspoon baking powder
> ¼ teaspoon salt
> ½ cup (1 stick) unsalted butter, chilled and cut into 8 tablespoon-size pieces
> 4 tablespoons margarine, chilled and cut into 4 pieces
> ¼ cup currants
> 1 large egg
> ¼ cup milk

Mix together the flour, ½ cup of the sugar, allspice, baking powder, and salt. Cut in half the butter (4 tablespoons) and all of the margarine until the mixture looks like coarse grains. (This can be done by hand with a pastry blender or in a food processor fitted with a metal blade.) Mix in the currants.

In a small bowl, combine the egg and milk. Make a well

in the center of the flour mixture and add the liquid. Mix well. (If you are using a food processor, pour the liquid through the feed tube and process until just combined, 15 to 20 seconds.)

Turn the dough out onto wax paper and divide into 4 equal portions. Divide each of these into 6 small balls, making 24 in all. Flatten each ball into 3-inch circles.

Melt one of the remaining tablespoons of butter in a heavy skillet over moderate heat. Add 4 dough circles and flatten them further with a floured spatula. Cook until golden brown, about 2 to 3 minutes per side. Transfer to a wire rack to cool, and sprinkle with some of the remaining sugar. Repeat with the remaining circles, butter, and sugar, flouring the spatula for each batch.

Yield: 24 cookies

ORANGE SHORTBREAD BISCUITS

This is another Sarah Leah Chase contribution to the enormous range of Celtic culinary delights. Ms. Chase has an instinct for dramatizing and intensifying the flavors of traditional foods, and these deeply citrus flavored cookies are a fine example of that talent. The recipe can be halved; the dough can also be frozen with no ill effects.

There are two schools of thought on the subject of shortbread: some like it thick (as this recipe is written); some like it thin and crisp. If you are a member of the latter school, simply roll these thinner and shorten the baking time.

2 cups (4 sticks) unsalted butter, softened
1½ cups brown sugar, firmly packed
4 cups unbleached flour
Pinch of salt
Finely grated zest of 2 oranges
2 large eggs
2 tablespoons water

Cream the butter and brown sugar in a mixing bowl. Gradually beat in the flour and salt to make a fairly stiff dough. Stir in the orange zest. Wrap the dough in plastic wrap or wax paper and refrigerate for at least 2 hours.

Preheat the oven to 350°. Line two baking sheets with parchment paper.

Turn the dough out onto a lightly floured board and roll to a thickness of ½ inch. Cut the dough with an assortment of 1½- to 2-inch cookie cutters and place on the prepared baking sheets.

Beat the eggs and water together in a small bowl and brush lightly over the cookies. Bake until light golden brown, about 15 to 20 minutes. (Or, if you prefer your cookies very crisp, bake until they are a deep golden brown, about 3 to 5 more minutes.) Let cool on wire racks, then store in airtight containers until ready to serve.

Yield: 60 cookies

SHORTBREAD FANS

Shortbread can be formed into lots of traditional shapes—I have seen recipes for shortbread in the form of seashells, for whole pie pans thickly packed with shortbread dough and scored into wedges, and for "petticoat tails." The latter are formed by flattening a circle of shortbread dough, removing a small circle of dough from the center, and cutting the rest of the dough into wedges. The resulting shape looks like a sewing pattern for a skirt or petticoat. These shortbread fans are similarly wedge-shaped, although, like a fan, they end in a point.

This basic recipe can also be made into a very rich shortbread known as a Pitcaithly Bannock by adding ¼ cup blanched, finely chopped almonds and 1 tablespoon caraway seeds.

> *1 cup (2 sticks) unsalted butter, softened*
> *¾ teaspoon salt*
> *¾ cup dark brown sugar, firmly packed*
> *2 cups flour*

Preheat the oven to 300°. Line two baking sheets with parchment paper and set aside.

Cream the butter in the bowl of an electric mixer or a food processor. Add the salt and sugar and beat until light and fluffy.

Add the flour, ⅓ cup at a time, until a soft dough is formed. (Do not overbeat!) Turn out the dough onto a floured or cornstarched board and divide into 4 portions.

Place two portions of dough on each baking sheet. Flatten each portion into a 5-inch round, score each into 6 wedges by pricking with the tines of a fork, and press the flat side of the tines around the edges of each round to make a decorative border.

Bake for 25 to 30 minutes, or until rounds are just firm to the touch. While the rounds are still warm, cut them along the fork marks without cutting all the way through. Let the cookies cool on the baking sheets, then break them into wedges.

Yield: 24 fan-shaped cookies

OATMEAL SHORTBREAD COOKIES

Many Scottish immigrants settled in eastern Canada, where their culinary traditions influenced other settlers. This excellent recipe comes from Canadian journalist and cooking school director Bonnie Stern, whose Aunt Reba used to make these cookies. But beware: like all good shortbreads, they can be seriously addictive!

1½ cups unbleached flour
½ teaspoon salt
1 teaspoon baking soda
1 cup (2 sticks) unsalted butter, softened
½ cup sugar
¾ cup light brown sugar, firmly packed
1 egg

½ teaspoon vanilla extract
½ teaspoon almond extract
½ cup chopped walnuts
2 cups rolled oats (not instant), ground in a food
  processor

Preheat oven to 350°. Grease two cookie sheets, or line with parchment paper, and set aside.

In a large bowl, mix together the flour, salt, and baking soda. In another large bowl, cream the butter with both sugars. In a small bowl, beat the egg and the extracts together. Then add the flour mixture to the butter mixture alternately with the beaten egg and extracts. Mix rapidly and only until just blended.

Combine the chopped walnuts and ground oatmeal (a food processor is ideal for this) and add them to the dough.

Form the dough into teaspoon-size balls. Drop the balls onto the prepared baking sheets and press down with a fork or the flat bottom of a glass dipped in flour. Cookies should be very thin and crisp.

Bake 8 to 12 minutes. Remove from sheets and cool on wire racks.

  Yield: 60 cookies

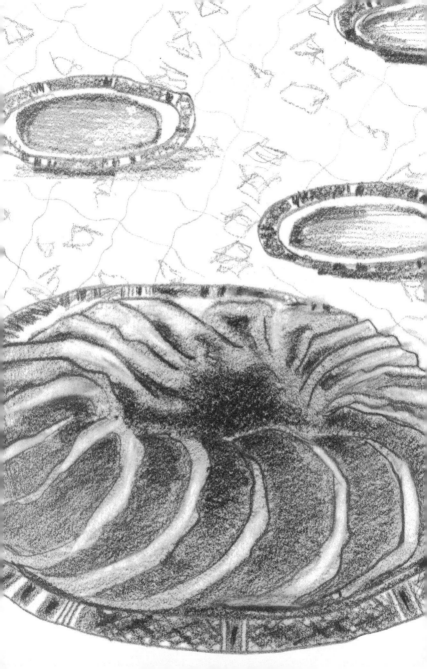

FESTIVE ENDINGS

Tea Cakes

and

Sweet Cakes

*I*n Ireland and all throughout the British Isles, the phrase "tea cakes" can often denote a cookie, or else small sweet scone-like griddle cakes; and the term "sweet cakes" could imply something much creamier and more sugary than the recipes collected here. In the United States, however, we call tea cakes those whole cakes that are sweeter than breads but less showy than gooey birthday affairs; and a sweet cake is more in a dessert-after-dinner class.

Within the range of sweet slices to go with coffee or tea (whether in the afternoon or evening), there are many variations. The tea cakes and sweet cakes that follow can all be served plain for tea, or after casual family meals, but I have also included various suggestions for amplifying their flavors and elevating their style into something more sophisticated and showy.

Each of these cakes is quite special, featuring a Celtic flair for intense flavor and unusual juxtapositions of textures. And, happily (except perhaps for the last entry, Black Bun), they are all extremely easy to prepare and bake.

IRISH BLACK GINGER CAKE

Gingerbreads, ginger biscuits, and ginger cakes are all traditional features of Celtic cooking. This particular cake—deep, dense, and dark, with a strong ginger and molasses flavor—is like a chocolate cake without the chocolate! It is very good plain, cut in thin slices or in bars. For a festive event, you may want to consider serving this with warm, thinned lemon curd or a hot lemon custard, or with whipped cream. The cake can also be split horizontally and frosted inside and out with a cream cheese frosting to which has been added the chopped zest of a lemon or an orange.

½ cup (1 stick) butter, softened
½ cup sugar
1 egg
1 cup blackstrap molasses
2½ cups unbleached flour
1½ teaspoons cinnamon
1 teaspoon ground cloves
1 teaspoon ground ginger
½ teaspoon salt
1½ teaspoons baking soda
1 cup hot strong freshly brewed coffee

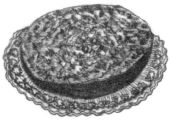

Preheat the oven to 350°. Butter an 8-inch square or 9-inch round cake pan and set aside.

Cream together the butter and sugar until smooth. In a large bowl, beat the egg into the molasses, then add to the butter mixture.

Sift together the flour, spices, and salt, then fold into the butter mixture.

Dissolve the baking soda in the hot coffee, then add it to the batter. Beat vigorously until well blended. Scrape the batter into the prepared pan.

Bake for 45 to 60 minutes, or until a tester inserted into the center of the cake comes out clean.

Yield: 1 single layer cake

TEA BRACK

Tea brack is a cross between a fruitcake and a bread. *Brack* means bread in Irish, and a barm brack (see page 40) is the more traditional yeasted version of this bread. But for its speed and ease, tea brack is worthy of inclusion. This version comes from Bernard Clayton.

> 2 cups mixed raisins and currants
> 1½ cups brown sugar, firmly packed
> 1½ cups cold strong tea
> ¼ cup rum
> 2 cups unbleached flour
> 1½ teaspoons baking powder
> ½ teaspoon cinnamon
> ½ teaspoon nutmeg
> ½ teaspoon salt
> 1 egg

Combine fruit, brown sugar, tea, and rum in a large mixing bowl, cover with plastic wrap or a plate, and let sit overnight at room temperature.

Preheat the oven to 325°. Grease an 8 × 4-inch loaf pan and set aside.

Into another mixing bowl, sift together the flour, baking

powder, cinnamon, nutmeg, and salt. Pour this dry mix-ture into the fruit mixture and stir well. Add the egg.

Scrape the dough into the prepared pan and bake 1½ hours, or until a cake tester pushed into the center comes out clean.

Set the pan on a wire rack and cool for 5 minutes. Turn the cake out of the pan and cool completely on the rack before cutting.

Confectioners sugar can be sifted over the top just before cutting.

Yield: 1 loaf

BLACK BUN

Extremely archaic-looking, Black Bun is indeed an antique, being a remnant from an old druidical cer-emony. Originally prepared as ritual food for the time of gathering in the mistletoe, it was also part of the ceremonial reward for those who took part in mum-mers' or guisers' plays. Today Black Bun is still a festive food for Hogmanay, the Scottish New Year.

Don't be put off by the large number of ingredients or the necessity for making a pie crust. This is really a very simple cake to make, with an inimitable taste and texture. If you have a mincemeat fancier in your household (as we do), it will disappear faster than you can first-foot into the New Year.

FOR THE PASTRY
3 cups sifted flour
¼ teaspoon salt
½ teaspoon baking powder
½ cup butter

FOR THE FILLING
1¼ pounds (4 cups) currants
12 ounces (2 cups) raisins
1 cup blanched and chopped almonds
1 cup chopped mixed candied (or dried) fruits
⅔ cups light brown sugar, firmly packed
2 cups sifted flour
¼ teaspoon salt
1½ teaspoons cinnamon
½ teaspoon ground ginger
¾ teaspoon allspice
½ teaspoon freshly ground black pepper
1½ teaspoons baking soda
1½ teaspoons cream of tartar
4 eggs
¼ cup brandy or milk
1 tablespoon cold water

Preheat the oven to 300°. Grease an 8-inch springform pan, which can be further lined with greased parchment paper if desired.

First, make the pastry. Sift together the flour, salt, and baking powder. Using a pastry blender or a food processor, cut the butter into the flour mixture until it is grainy. Add just enough water to make a stiff dough (in a processor, the dough should form a ragged mass that rides the blade).

Reserve ⅓ of the dough for the top of the pastry. Turn out the remaining ⅔ of the dough onto a floured board and roll into a 12-inch circle. Line bottom and sides of the prepared pan with this circle of dough. Set aside.

Then make the filling. In a very large mixing bowl, combine the currants, raisins, almonds, fruits, and sugar. In a smaller bowl, mix together the flour, salt, cinnamon, ginger, allspice, pepper, baking soda, and cream of tartar, then add to the fruit mixture.

Beat 3 of the eggs lightly and add them, with the brandy or milk, to the flour mixture. Using your hands, dig in and mix well until the whole mass is well moistened.

Fill the pastry-lined pan with this filling. Roll out the reserved dough into a 9-inch round and fit it loosely over the cake. Secure the edges by pinching together decoratively. (The edges can be moistened with water to make them stick more easily.)

Beat the remaining egg and mix with the water. Brush the top of the cake with this egg wash. Using a skewer or a chopstick, prick three or four holes down through the top pastry and to the bottom of the filling.

Bake for 2½ to 3 hours, or until a cake tester inserted into the center comes out clean. Remove the cake from the pan and cool on a rack. Brandy may be poured, drop by drop, through the holes in the bun as it cools.

Cut into thin wedges and serve. Lily-gilders might want whipped cream, hard sauce, or ice cream.

Yield: 1 large pie-shaped cake

PORTER CAKE

Porter is strong ale, and dark stout is often the closest substitute available in many parts of the United States. But this cake, whether you call it stout or porter, is memorable however it is made. Baked in a large tube pan, it offers many generous servings.

> 4 cups self-rising flour (see page 25)
> ½ teaspoon salt
> 2 cups sugar
> 1 teaspoon freshly grated nutmeg
> 1 teaspoon allspice
> 1 cup (2 sticks) butter
> Grated zest of 1 lemon
> Grated zest of 1 orange
> 2 cups golden raisins
> 1 12-ounce bottle Guinness stout
> 2 eggs, beaten

Preheat the oven to 300°. Grease and flour a 9½-inch tube or Bundt pan and set aside.

Sift together the flour, salt, sugar, nutmeg, and allspice.

Cut in the butter with a pastry blender until the mixture looks like coarse meal. Add the citrus zests and raisins and mix until the fruit is well distributed.

Combine the stout with the beaten eggs and add to the dough, mixing well.

Scrape the batter into the prepared pan and bake for 2½ hours, or until a tester inserted in the center of the cake comes out clean. Turn out and cool on a wire rack; do not cut until completely cooled.

Serve plain, with confectioner's sugar sifted over the top, or with whipped cream.

Yield: 24 servings

DUNDEE CAKE

There are many recipes for Dundee Cake, a Scottish fruitcake, and at least one of them must be awful, judging from Laurie Colwin's story of an unsuccessful festive dessert in her book *Home Cooking*. This recipe, however, can be relied upon to taste both wonderful and authentic, thanks to Craig Claiborne's careful adaptation for American ingredients.

1 cup sultanas or raisins
½ cup currants
¾ cup (1½ sticks) unsalted butter, softened
¾ cup sugar
3 eggs
2¼ cups sifted flour
1 teaspoon baking powder
½ teaspoon salt
½ cup milk
Shredded rind of 1 small orange
¼ cup chopped blanched almonds
10–12 blanched almonds, split, for garnish

Grease a 9-inch springform pan or casserole. Line the bottom with greased wax paper or parchment and set aside. Preheat the oven to 325°.

Chop the raisins and mix them with the currants. Place in a small bowl and set aside.

Whip the butter well. Add the sugar gradually and whip until fluffy. Add the eggs one at a time, beating until very fluffy after each addition.

Sift together the flour, baking powder, and salt. Add this flour mixture and milk alternately to the butter mixture, stirring after each addition only until mixed. Do not beat.

Fold in the fruit mixture and orange rind and add the

chopped almonds. Pour into the prepared pan and arrange the split almonds over the top in a decorative pattern.

Bake about 1¼ hours or until the cake has begun to shrink from the sides of the pan. Cool 15 minutes before removing from the pan.

Yield: 1 round loaf

TREACLE PARKIN

This cake has not only a wonderful name but a most wonderful flavor as well—a taste like mocha mixed with butterscotch. It is quite simple to make, and is a good candidate for a child's baking project. It can be decorated with powdered sugar sifted through a paper doily, or it can be iced with any white frosting.

1½ cups dark brown sugar, firmly packed
1 cup (2 sticks) unsalted butter, softened
2 cups unbleached flour
2 tablespoons ground ginger
1 tablespoon cinnamon
1 cup molasses
2 eggs, lightly beaten

1 teaspoon baking soda
½ cup scalded milk

Preheat the oven to 325°. Butter and flour an 11¾ ×
7½-inch baking pan or an 8- 9-inch-square cake pan.

Cream the brown sugar and the butter together until
fluffy. Sift together the flour and spices. Combine the
molasses and eggs and add to the butter mixture alternately with the flour mixture.

Dissolve the baking soda in the hot milk and stir into the
batter. Pour batter into the prepared pan and bake for
1½ hours, or until a cake tester inserted into the center
comes out clean.

Let the cake cool in the pan for 10 minutes, then turn
out onto a rack to cool completely.

Serve plain, sugared, or iced.

*Yield: 1 rectangular
sheet cake*

BIBLIOGRAPHY

BEARD, JAMES. *Beard on Bread*. New York: *Alfred A. Knopf*, 1974.

BROWN, CATHERINE. *Scottish Cookery*. Glasgow: *Richard Drew Publishing*, 1989.

CHASE, SARAH LEAH. *Nantucket Open House Cookbook*. New York: *Workman Publishing*, 1987.

CLAIBORNE, CRAIG. *The New York Times Cookbook*. New York: *Harper & Row*, 1961.

——. *The New York Times Menu Cookbook*. New York: *Harper & Row*, 1966.

CLAYTON, BERNARD. *Bernard Clayton's New Complete Book of Breads*. New York: *Simon & Schuster*, 1987.

COLWIN, LAURIE. *Home Cooking*. New York: *Alfred A. Knopf*, 1988.

DAVID, ELIZABETH. *English Bread and Yeast Cookery*. Introduction and American adaptations by Karen Hess. New York: *Viking Penguin*, 1980.

DAVIES, GILLI. *Lamb, Leeks, and Laverbread: The Best of Welsh Cookery*. London: *Grafton Books, Collins Publishing Group*, 1989.

FITZGIBBON, THEODORA. *A Taste of Ireland*. London: Pan Books Ltd., 1971.

——. *A Taste of Scotland*. London: *Pan Books Ltd*, 1971.

——. *Irish Traditional Food*. London: *Pan Books Ltd*, 1984.

FREY, IRIS IHDE. *Crumpets and Scones.* New York: *St. Martin's Press,* 1982.

GRIGSON, JANE. *Jane Grigson's British Cookery.* New York: *Atheneum,* 1984.

HOPE, ANNETTE. *A Caledonian Feast.* Edinburgh: *Mainstream Publishing Co.,* 1987.

HYNES, ANGELA. *The Pleasures of Afternoon Tea.* Tucson, Ariz.: *HP Books,* 1987.

McCORMICK, MALACHI. *Malachi McCormick's Irish Country Cooking.* New York: *Clarkson N. Potter,* 1988.

MOOSEWOOD COLLECTIVE. *New Moosewood Cookbook.* Berkeley, Calif.: *Ten Speed Press,* 1987.

STERN, BONNIE. *Bonnie Stern's Cuisinart Cookbook.* Toronto: *Madison Press Books,* 1984.

TIBBOTT, S. MINWELL. *Cooking on the Open Hearth.* Wales: *National Museum of Wales, Welsh Folk Museum,* 1982.

INDEX

Grateful acknowledgment is made for permission to use the following recipes:

Currant and caraway scones and orange shortbread from *Nantucket Open House Cookbook* by Sarah Leah Chase. © 1987 by Sarah Leah Chase. Reprinted by permission of Workman Publishing Company Inc. All rights reserved.

Dundee cake from *New York Times Cookbook* by Craig Claiborne. Copyright © 1961 by Craig Claiborne. Reprinted by permission of HarperCollins Publishers.

Black bun from *New York Times Menu Cookbook* by Craig Claiborne. Copyright © 1966 by The New York Times Company. Reprinted by permission of HarperCollins Publishers.

Ten selections from *The Complete Book of Breads* by Bernard Clayton, Jr. Copyright © 1973, 1987 by Bernard Clayton, Jr. Reprinted by permission of Simon & Schuster, Inc.

Bara gwenith and teisennau ffair llanddarog from *Lamb, Leeks and Laverbread* by Gilli Davies. Copyright Gilli Davies, 1989. Reprinted by permission of the author and Grafton Books, a division of HarperCollins Publishers Limited.

Soda bread from *British Cookery* by Jane Grigson. Copyright © 1984 by Jane Grigson. Reprinted with permission of Atheneum Publishers, an imprint of Macmillan Publishing Company.

Pratie oaten from *Malachi McCormick's Irish Country Cooking* by Malachi McCormick. Copyright © 1988 by Malachi McCormick. Reprinted by permission of Clarkson N. Potter, Inc., a division of Crown Publishers, Inc.

Oatmeal shortbread cookies from *Bonnie Stern's Cuisinart Cookbook*. Courtesy of Bonnie Stern.